SUPER SOCIAL STUDIES INFOGRAPHICS

US GEOGRAPHY THROUGH INFOGRAPHICS

Nadia Higgins

graphics by
Laura Westlund

Lerner Publications Company
Minneapolis

Note: Some graphs include rounded percentages. Because of this, not all totals will equal 100 percent.

Lerner Publications Company
A division of Lerner Publishing Group, Inc.
241 First Avenue North
Minneapolis, MN 55401 USA

For reading levels and more information, look up this title at www.lernerbooks.com.

Main text set in Univers LT Std 12/15.
Typeface provided by Adobe Systems.

Library of Congress Cataloging-in-Publication Data

Higgins, Nadia.
US geography through infographics / by Nadia Higgins.
pages cm.
Includes index.
ISBN 978-1-4677-3462-2 (lib. bdg. : alk. paper)
ISBN 978-1-4677-4747-9 (eBook)
1. Geography—Study and teaching (Elementary)—United States. 2. Communication in geography—Graphic methods. 3. Information visualization. 4. Visual communication. I. Title.
G76.5.U6H54 2014
917.3—dc23 2013036156

Manufactured in the United States of America
1 – PC – 7/15/14

CONTENTS

GOING PLACES

Do you have a future as a geographer? To find out, take this test!

1. Do you like knowing your exact location—and the route you took to get there?

2. Do you ever think about why things are where they are?

3. Do you notice trends in your school and in society?

4. Are you mesmerized by maps?

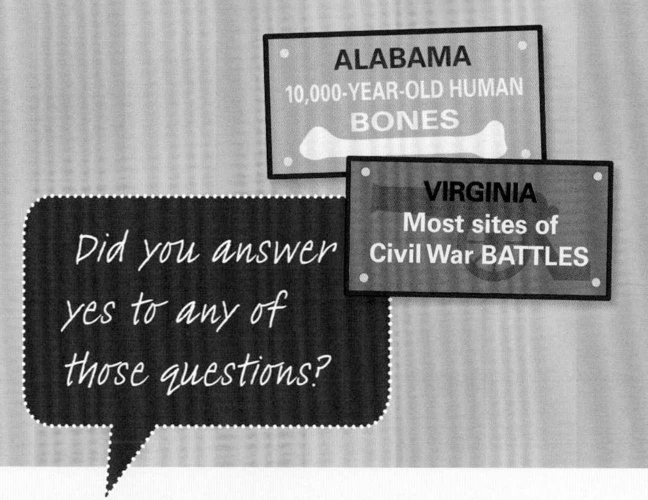

CONGRATULATIONS!

You have what it takes to be a geographer of the United States of America. US geographers are interested in places—from cities and states to the country as a whole. They examine our country's land, nature, and people. They also study how these three forces move, change, and interact.

That's a lot to keep straight! Geographers use maps, graphs, and other infographics to keep their info clear and organized. Are you ready to join in the fun? Let's get started!

HOW WE RANK

"We're number 1!" The United States is known as the world's superpower. But in what ways do we really rank at the top? And is being first always a good thing? Take a look at how the United States stacks up to nearly 200 other countries in the world.

1st

Oil consumed:
18.5 million barrels per day

Number of airports:
15,079

Roadways:
4 million miles (6.5 million kilometers)

Total wealth:
about $16 trillion in 2012

Millionaires:
3.1 million

2nd

Coal mined:
more than 1 billion tons (0.9 billion metric tons) a year

Climate change contribution:
more than 7 billion tons (6.7 billion metric tons) of greenhouse gases per year

3rd

Physical size:
3,794,100 square miles (9,826,675 sq. km)

Population:

million

123rd

Rate of population growth: up about 1 percent each year

60th

Money spent on education: 5.4 percent of the nation's total wealth

51st

Average length of life: 78.6 years

6th

CLEANEST AIR

18 on a measure from 11 to 279 by the World Health Organization

12th

IMMIGRANTS

12 percent of the population was born in another country

14th

Average wealth per person: $50,700

BREAK IT DOWN

Geographers have dozens of ways of dividing the United States into regions. They look at shared traits such as climate, land, and the natural environment. They also look at culture (the traits and customs of a people) and history. The regions in the map here take all those factors into consideration. As usual, Alaska and Hawaii stand alone.

AND THE AWARD GOES TO...

coldest

Barrow, Alaska: average temperature 11.7°F (-11°C)

snowiest

Valdez, Alaska: 27 feet (8 m) of snow per year

27 feet (8 m)

Juneau

Honolulu

wettest

Hilo, Hawaii: 126.7 inches (3.2 m) of rain per year

driest hottest

Death Valley, California: often 120°F (49°C) in summer; gets only about 2.5 inches (0.06 m) of rain per year

Olympia, Washington

Salem, Oregon

Sacramento, California

PACIFIC COAST

Climate: mild all year round; winter drizzle

Land: rugged shores, mountains, evergreen forests, semidesert

Animal sighting: sea lion

Backyard plant: western juniper tree

Known for: earthquakes, lots of high-tech jobs

Sante Fe, New Mexico

Phoenix, Arizona

Climate: dry and hot

Land: desert, red rock landscapes

Animal sighting: nine-banded armadillo

Backyard plant: bunny ears cactus

ROCKY MOUNTAIN

Climate: varies by elevation, from dry and sunny to cold and snowy

Land: majestic mountains, deserts, high plateaus

Animal sighting: elk

Backyard plant: columbine and other wildflowers

Known for: world-class skiing and white-water rafting

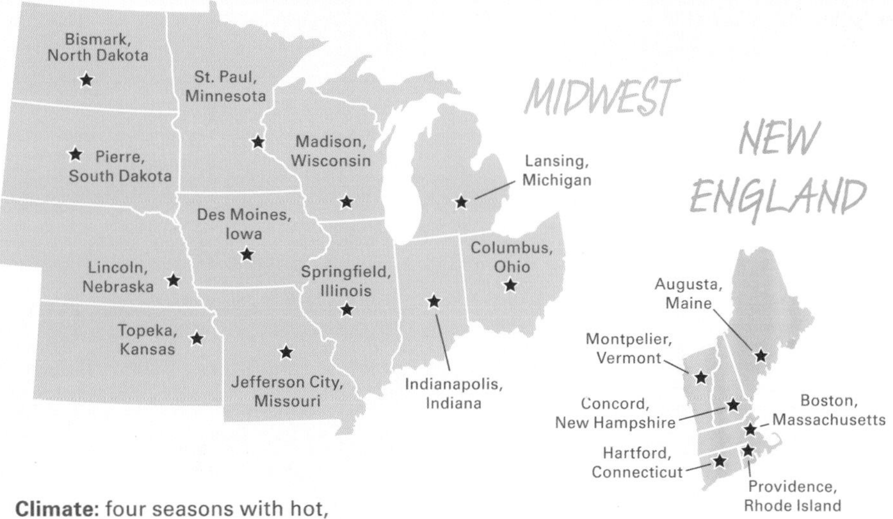

MIDWEST

Climate: four seasons with hot, humid summers and harsh winters

Land: rolling prairies, lots of lakes

Animal sighting: prairie dog

Backyard plant: peony

Known for: farms that stretch as far as the eye can see

NEW ENGLAND

Climate: four distinct seasons with warm summers and snowy winters

Land: coastlines, rocky hills, and fertile valleys

Animal sighting: basking shark

Backyard plant: sugar maple tree

Known for: quaint villages and harbors

MID-ATLANTIC

Climate: hot, humid summers and cold winters; milder in DE, MD, and DC

Land: coastline, wetlands, low mountains

Animal sighting: red-bellied woodpecker

Backyard plant: New York ironweed

Known for: lots of busy cities

Albany, New York
Harrisburg, Pennsylvania
Trenton, New Jersey
Washington, DC
Annapolis, Maryland
Dover, Delaware

SOUTH

Charleston, West Virginia
Frankfort, Kentucky
Nashville, Tennessee
Richmond, Virginia
Little Rock, Arkansas
Raleigh, North Carolina
Atlanta, Georgia
Columbia, South Carolina
Baton Rouge, Louisiana
Jackson, Mississippi
Montgomery, Alabama
Tallahassee, Florida

Climate: long, hot, sticky summers and mild winters

Land: sandy beaches, fertile plains, and long mountain trails

Animal sighting: American alligator

Backyard plant: azalea

Known for: beach resorts; hospitality

SOUTHWEST

Oklahoma City, Oklahoma
Austin, Texas

Known for: artist communities; food influenced by Mexican flavors

YOUR LAND, MY LAND

Majestic mountains, eerie deserts, lush forests, endless prairie. . . The United States offers a breathtaking array of landscapes. The natural features of each region shape what life is like there. What industries are in your area? What kinds of natural disasters strike? Natural features help answer those questions—and many more.

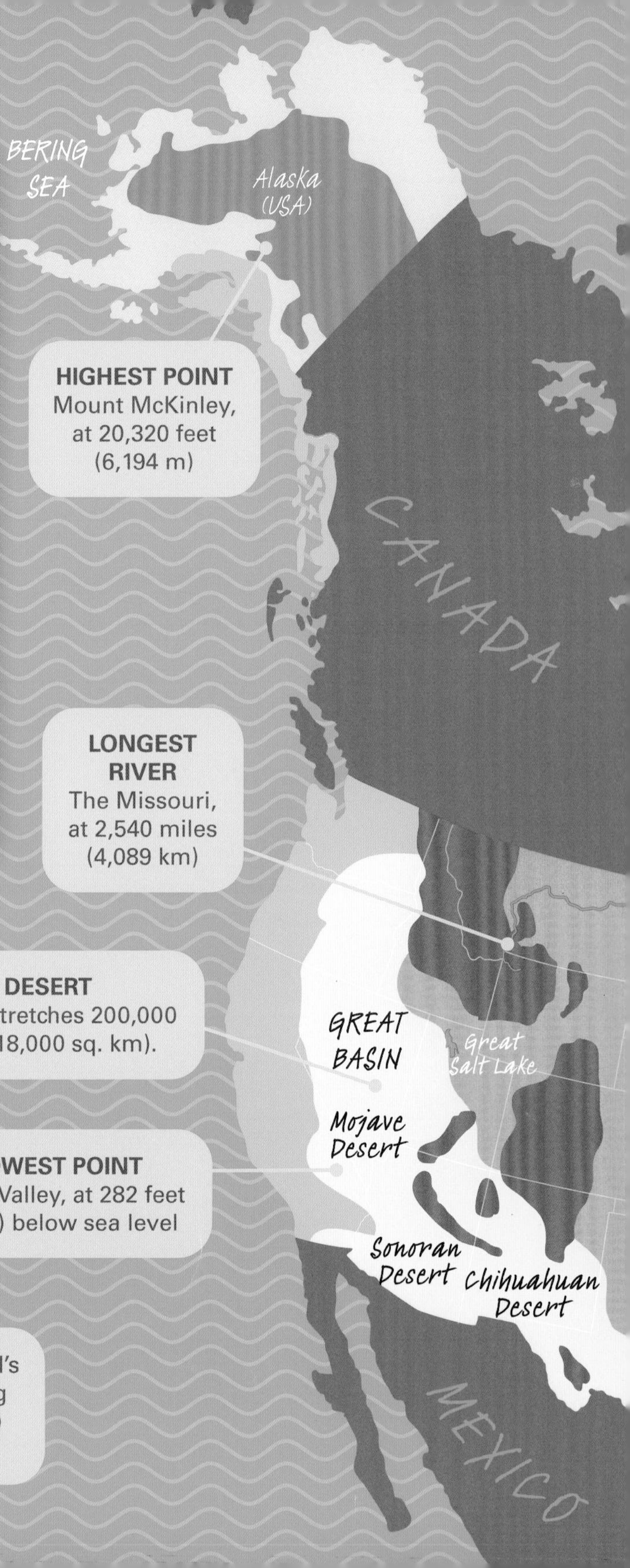

HIGHEST POINT
Mount McKinley, at 20,320 feet (6,194 m)

LONGEST RIVER
The Missouri, at 2,540 miles (4,089 km)

LARGEST DESERT
The Great Basin stretches 200,000 square miles (518,000 sq. km).

LOWEST POINT
Death Valley, at 282 feet (86 m) below sea level

Mauna Loa is the world's biggest volcano, rising 56,000 feet (17,000 m) from the ocean floor.

USE IT WISELY

Major land uses in the United States:

The gently rolling grasslands of the Great Plains stretch into more than 10 states.

The Great Lakes hold 90 percent of the country's freshwater supply.

Lake Superior

Lake Michigan

Lake Huron

Lake Ontario

Lake Erie

GREAT PLAINS

ATLANTIC COASTAL PLAIN

GULF COASTAL PLAIN

ATLANTIC OCEAN

GULF OF MEXICO

REGIONS OF THE US

- Mountain
- Tropical forest
- Plains
- Desert
- Deciduous forest
- Evergreen forest
- Polar

WHAT'S YOUR STATE'S CLAIM TO FAME?

It's time to play the license plate game! Check out what your state slogan might be if only geographers were in charge.

ALABAMA
10,000-YEAR-OLD HUMAN BONES

ALASKA
BIGGEST STATE

ARIZONA
MOST SUN

CALIFORNIA
MOST PEOPLE

COLORADO
Three-billion-year-old ROCKS

CONNECTICUT
Highest average household INCOME

HAWAII
Highest % of CARPOOLERS

IDAHO
3,000-YEAR-OLD TREE

INDIANA
More than 100 kinds of TREES

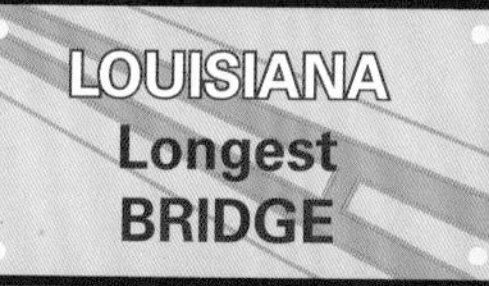

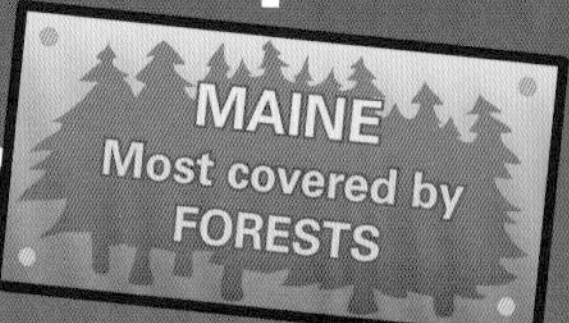

MARYLAND
No.1 for SAILING

MASSACHUSETTS
Most advanced DEGREES

MICHIGAN
#1 for transplanting ORGANS

MINNESOTA
Land of
10,000 LAKES

MISSISSIPPI
More places to go
to CHURCH

MISSOURI
EIGHT neighboring
states

MONTANA
Leads in dinosaur
FOSSILS

NEBRASKA
23,000 miles
(37,000 km)
of RIVERS

NEVADA
DRIEST

NEW HAMPSHIRE
Famous fall
FOLIAGE

NEW JERSEY
HORSE people
paradise

NEW MEXICO
More than 1 million
CATTLE

NEW YORK
SUBWAY system
No. 1 in size

NORTH CAROLINA
Home of the
SWEET POTATO

NORTH DAKOTA
OIL BOOM

OHIO
Most AMISH

OKLAHOMA
World's largest
protected PRAIRIE

OREGON
DEEPEST
lake

PENNSYLVANIA
OLDEST ZOO

RHODE ISLAND
No. 1 in TINY

SOUTH CAROLINA
Soft sand
BEACHES

SOUTH DAKOTA
Land of wild
TURKEYS

TENNESSEE
More than 9,600
CAVES

TEXAS
TORNADO
capital

UTAH
huge
SALTWATER lake

VERMONT
Cleanest AIR

VIRGINIA
Most sites of
Civil War BATTLES

WASHINGTON
GREEN energy
leader

WEST VIRGINIA
FLYING SQUIRREL
capital

WISCONSIN
More than 600 kinds
of CHEESE

WYOMING
Leads in
COAL

ON THE MOVE

One-fifth of all the cars in the world zip over US roads and highways. Driving is definitely the number one way of getting around our 50 states. But Americans are also known to fly, float, and even pedal along. Let's take a closer look at how we travel by air, land, and water.

IN THE SKY

GETTING TO WORK

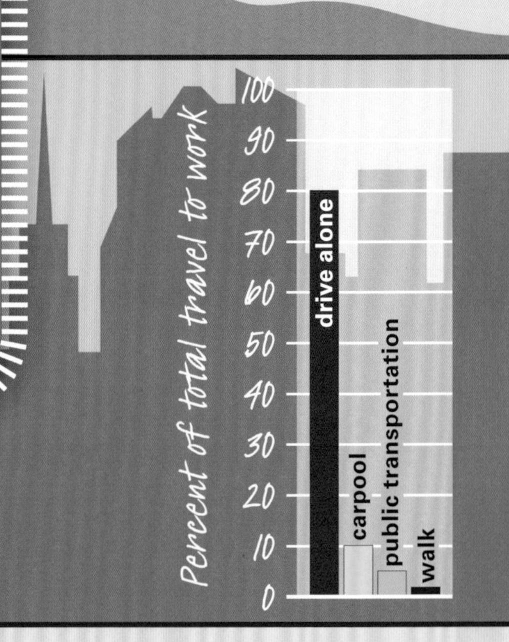

GETTING TO SCHOOL

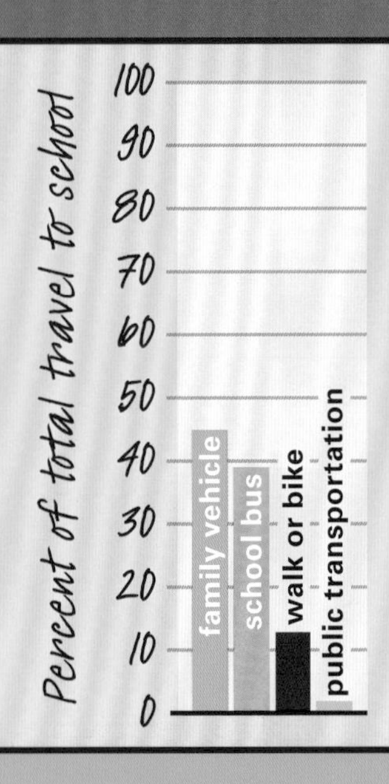

Just 2 percent of kids get to school by public transportation.

About 13 percent of kids in grades K through 8 walk or bike to school.

ON WATER

Ships and barges are the cheapest way to move goods.

barge

Airplanes handle 10 percent of all passenger travel.

Percent of total travel

all other means of transportation

commercial airlines

0 10 20 30 40 50 60 70 80 90 100

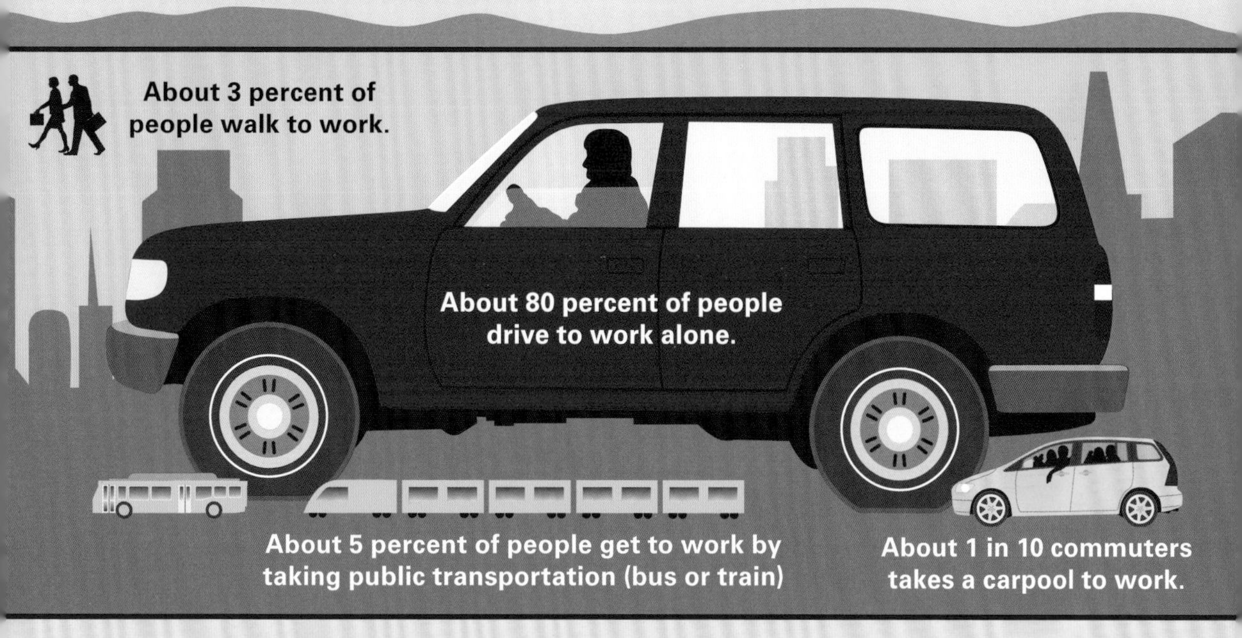

About 3 percent of people walk to work.

About 80 percent of people drive to work alone.

About 5 percent of people get to work by taking public transportation (bus or train)

About 1 in 10 commuters takes a carpool to work.

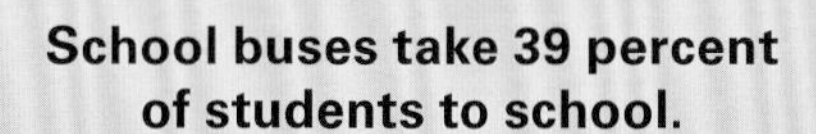

School buses take 39 percent of students to school.

About 45 percent of kids get a ride to school in their family vehicle.

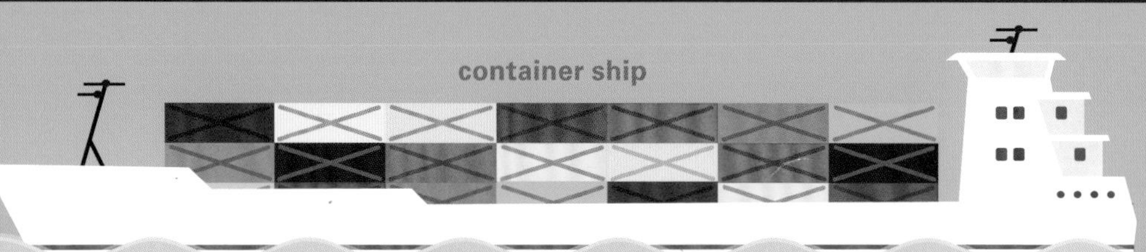

ROAD TRIP!

From snowy peaks to creepy caves, the United States offers a mind-blowing array of natural wonders. Next time you take a family road trip, maybe you can be in charge of the route. An amazing sight is just a drive away.

CRATER LAKE, OREGON

What it is: the deepest lake in the United States
How it formed: the top of a volcano caved in, leaving a crater that filled with water
Why we love it: mountains reflected in crystal clear water

GRAND CANYON, ARIZONA

What it is: an enormous canyon with striped rocky walls
How it formed: the Colorado River carved it out over milions of years
Why we love it: breathtaking views and plunges that make your knees weak

DELICATE ARCH, UTAH

What it is: a natural stone arch as high as a four-story building
How it formed: wind and rain carved away sandstone rock
Why we love it: just one of 2,500 stone arches in Arches National Park

MOUNT MCKINLEY, ALASKA

What it is: the tallest mountain in North America
How it formed: shifting tectonic plates (pieces of Earth's crust) folded the land into mountains
Why we love it: jaw-dropping cliff on the north side of the mountain

DEVIL'S TOWER, WYOMING

What it is: a towering, ridged rock formation
How it formed: magma (melted rock) bubbled up from inside Earth and cooled into hard, igneous rock. Then sedimentary rock around it wore away.
Why we love it: rock climbers scaling it like colorful bugs

NIAGARA FALLS, NEW YORK

What it is: huge, roaring waterfalls
How it formed: at the end of the last ice age, melting water streamed into Niagara River. The rushing river continues to wear away the gorge beneath the falls.
Why we love it: awesome clouds of mist

CAPE HATTERAS NATIONAL SEASHORE, NORTH CAROLINA

What it is: a string of barrier islands just off the coast
How it formed: storms, waves, changing sea levels, and wind shaped the islands—and continue to do so
Why we love it: home to several endangered species, including sea turtles

MAMMOTH CAVE, KENTUCKY

What it is: the world's longest cave
How it formed: acidic water trickled through the cracks in limestone, eventually carving the cracks into caves
Why we love it: underground lakes with eyeless fish

JOHN PENNEKAMP CORAL REEF STATE PARK, FLORIDA

What it is: an underwater ecosystem centered on living coral
How it formed: those colorful "rocky" reefs are actually the skeletons of tiny animals
Why we love it: 260 species of tropical fish

DISASTER ZONES

From floods to fires, just about every kind of natural disaster strikes in the United States. Let's look at risk zones for three of the deadliest.

In 1925, the deadliest tornado in US history killed 695 people in Missouri, Illinois, and Indiana. Its path is still a record breaker, at 219 miles (352 km) long.

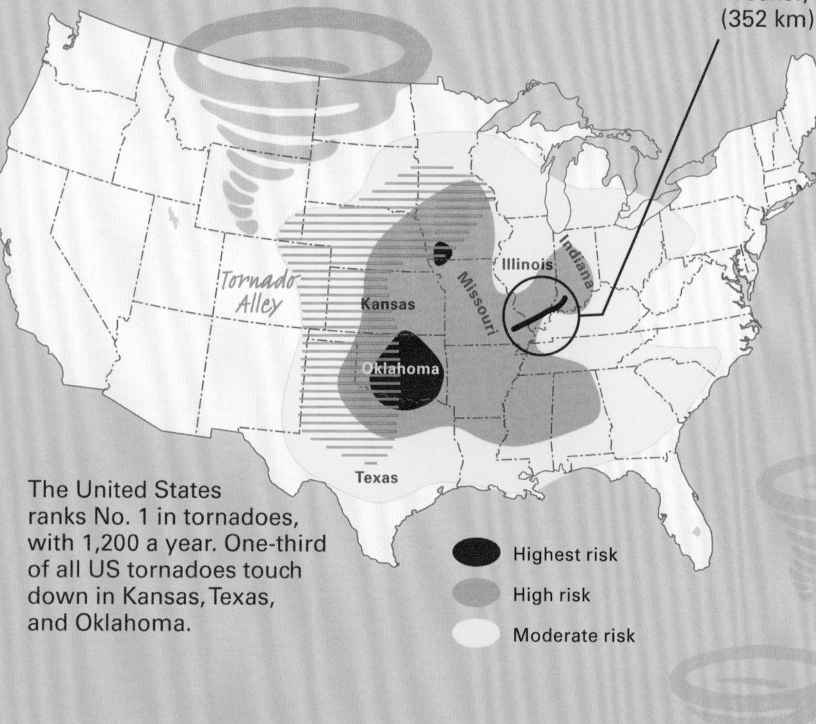

The United States ranks No. 1 in tornadoes, with 1,200 a year. One-third of all US tornadoes touch down in Kansas, Texas, and Oklahoma.

AWESOME SUCKING POWER

Tornadoes are spinning columns of air that drop down from severe thunderstorms. Tornadoes work like giant vacuum cleaners, sucking up dirt and objects in their path.

More tornadoes spin across Tornado Alley than any other place on Earth. In this area, warm, moist air streams north from the Gulf of Mexico. Meanwhile, cool, dry air rushes in from the Rockies. That combo makes for intense thunderstorms—and fierce tornadoes.

The deadliest hurricane in US history thrashed Galveston, Texas, in 1900. It left 8,000 people dead.

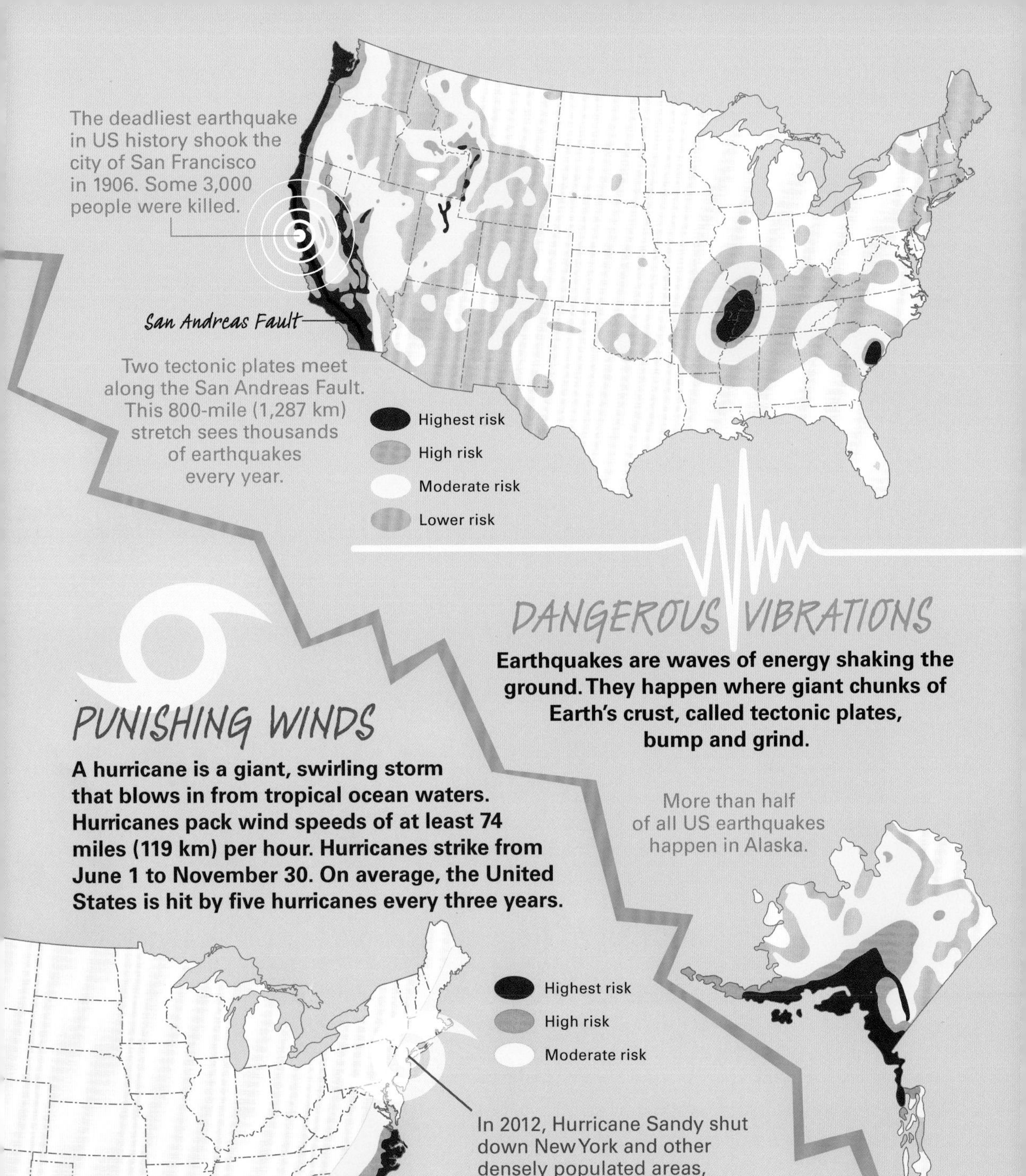

DANGEROUS VIBRATIONS

Earthquakes are waves of energy shaking the ground. They happen where giant chunks of Earth's crust, called tectonic plates, bump and grind.

PUNISHING WINDS

A hurricane is a giant, swirling storm that blows in from tropical ocean waters. Hurricanes pack wind speeds of at least 74 miles (119 km) per hour. Hurricanes strike from June 1 to November 30. On average, the United States is hit by five hurricanes every three years.

In 1935, the Florida Keys saw the most powerful hurricane in US history. Winds topped 155 miles (249 km) per hour.

ENERGY IN, ENERGY OUT

Check out the news today, and you'll probably see somebody worrying about energy. They mean *energy* as a natural resource—for example, oil to power cars or coal to make electricity. Energy presents two main problems in the United States: 1) Oil, coal, and natural gas still provide most of our energy, even though they contribute to climate change. 2) Americans use more energy than we can produce. We rely on other countries for 19 percent of our fuel.

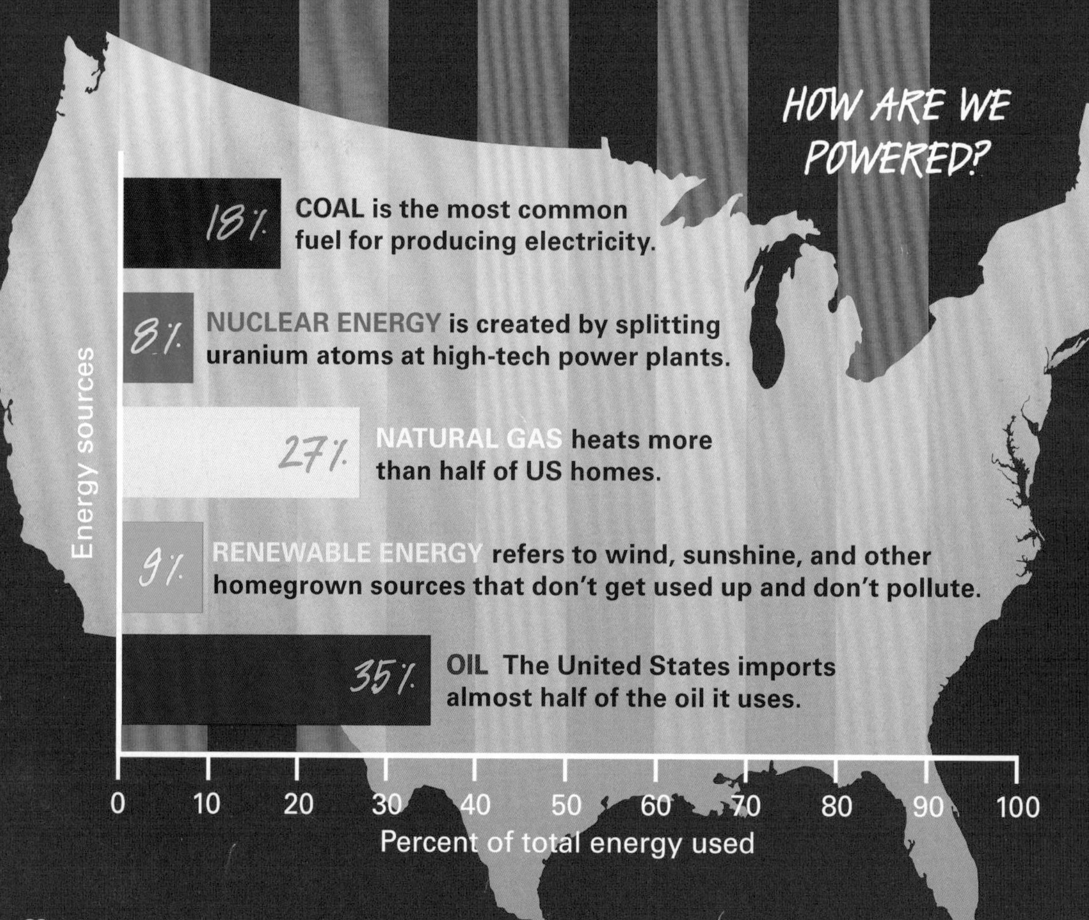

ENERGY TOP FIVES

PRODUCER POWERHOUSES

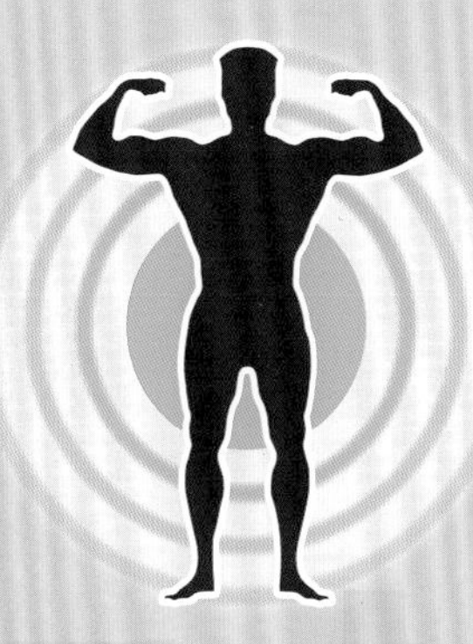

1. Texas
2. Wyoming
3. Louisiana
4. Pennsylvania
5. West Virginia

RENEWABLE ENERGY STARS

1. Washington
2. California
3. Oregon
4. Texas
5. New York

LOWEST ENERGY USE PER PERSON

1. Rhode Island
2. New York
3. Connecticut
4. Hawaii
5. California

HOW IS ENERGY USED?

The power we use at home is just a fraction of US energy use.

19% Businesses

28% Transportation (travel and shipping)

31% Industry (farms, factories, and mines)

22% Homes

CLIMATE CHANGE AT HOME

Imagine you've been out on a summer day. It's warm but not hot—until you get into your car. Your seat is scorching! That's because sunlight streamed into your car, and the windows trapped the heat energy inside. That same process is happening to our planet. In Earth's case, greenhouse gases are trapping the sun's heat inside the atmosphere. Those gases come from burning fossil fuels, such as coal and oil.

In the United States, the average temperature has risen more than 2°F (1.1°C) in the past 50 years. That heat is affecting rainfall, storm patterns, and other climate events. In turn, our physical and natural world is also changing in troubling ways.

COASTS

Change: polar ice melting, sea levels rising

One concern: storms and tides causing flooding in US cities, especially sewer flooding

HAWAII

Change: tropical ocean waters becoming warmer

One concern: harm to coral reefs and the many kinds of fish they support

SOUTHWEST

Change: longer, hotter periods of drought

One concern: increased wildfires

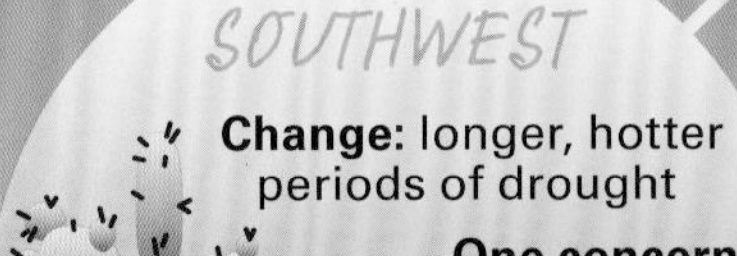

PACIFIC OCEAN

Why Scientists Are Worried

ALASKA

Change: winter temperature increasing by more than 6°F (3.3°C)

One concern: insect life cycles speeding up, causing insect outbreaks

MIDWEST

Change: heat waves getting hotter, longer, and more frequent

One concern: health threats from high temps and poor air quality

ROCKY MOUNTAINS

Change: animal and plant species moving up the mountain to cooler climates

One concern: nonnative species breaking up ecosystems, spelling the end of bighorn sheep and others

NORTHWEST

Change: more winter rain instead of snow

One concern: possible harm to salmon life cycle from changing water levels in streams

GREAT LAKES

Change: lakes evaporating, lower levels by the end of the century

One concern: dry docks and harbors

NORTHEAST

Change: heavy downpours already up 67 percent

One concern: pounding rains that wear away soil

ATLANTIC OCEAN

GULF OF MEXICO

SOUTH/SOUTHEAST

Change: more frequent hurricanes and more powerful hurricanes

One concern: costly damage to homes and businesses

WHERE WE LIVE

How far away are your neighbors? Are they one door down the hall? Or do you drive past miles of fields to see them? Check out how 317 million US citizens are spread out across the country.

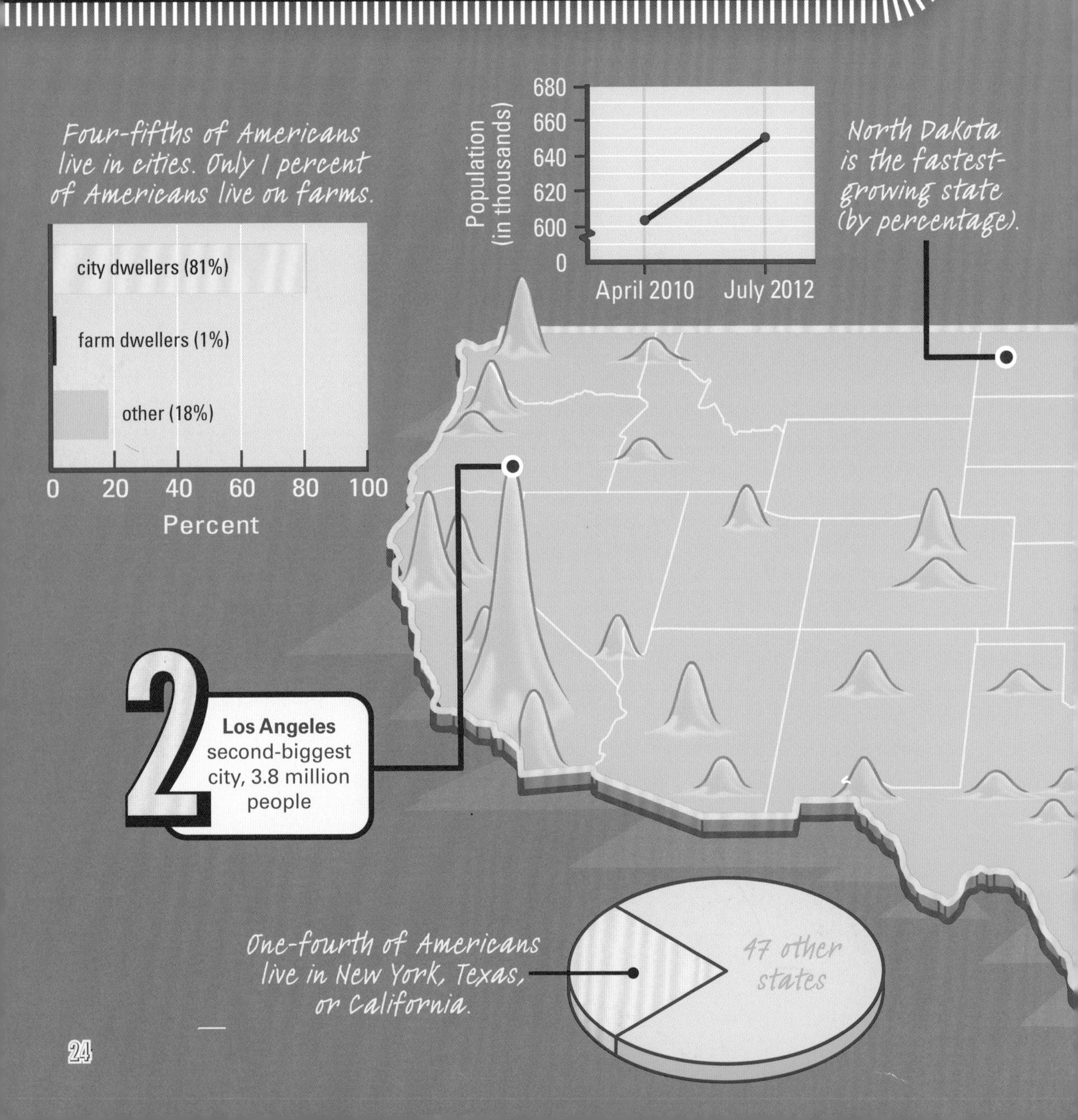

TWO EXTREMES

Alaska has miles of open space . . .

while New Jersey is the most crowded.

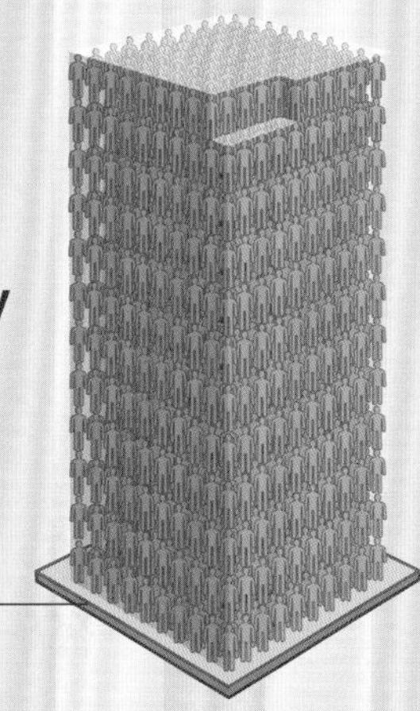

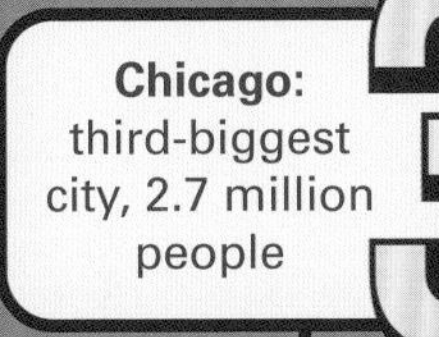

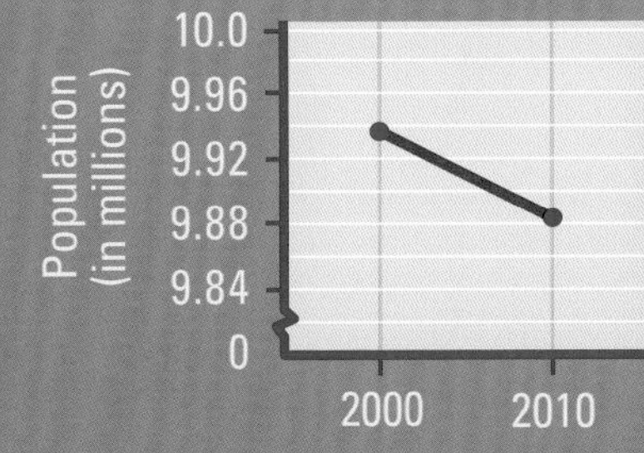

New York: largest city, 8.2 million people

Michigan is the only state where the population is going down.

Philadelphia: fifth-biggest city, 1.5 million people

Houston: fourth-biggest city, 2 million people

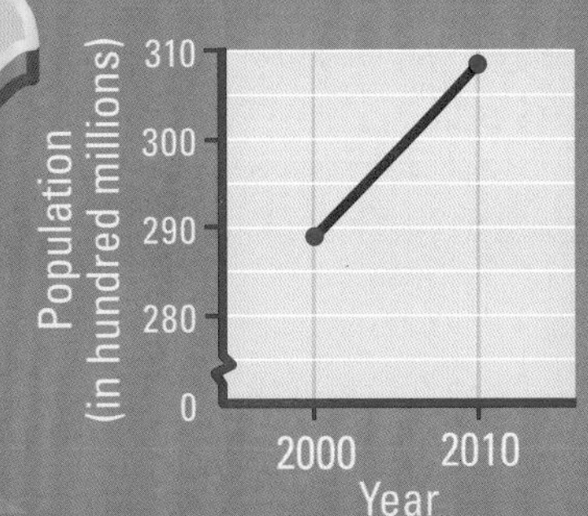

The US population grew by 10 percent between 2000 and 2010, mostly in the South and the West.

ALL-AMERICAN GRAPH-OUT!

Geographers are always on the lookout for patterns among people. How does a population break down according to sex, age, education level, and other factors? How are those factors connected, and how do they change over time? No doubt, geographers love maps. But sometimes a graph is just the tool for laying out the data.

Females vs. Males, by Age

This pyramid graph shows how old Americans are while comparing numbers of males and females. Turns out, preschoolers and people over 75 pair up almost one to one. Women start outnumbering men around the age of 60.

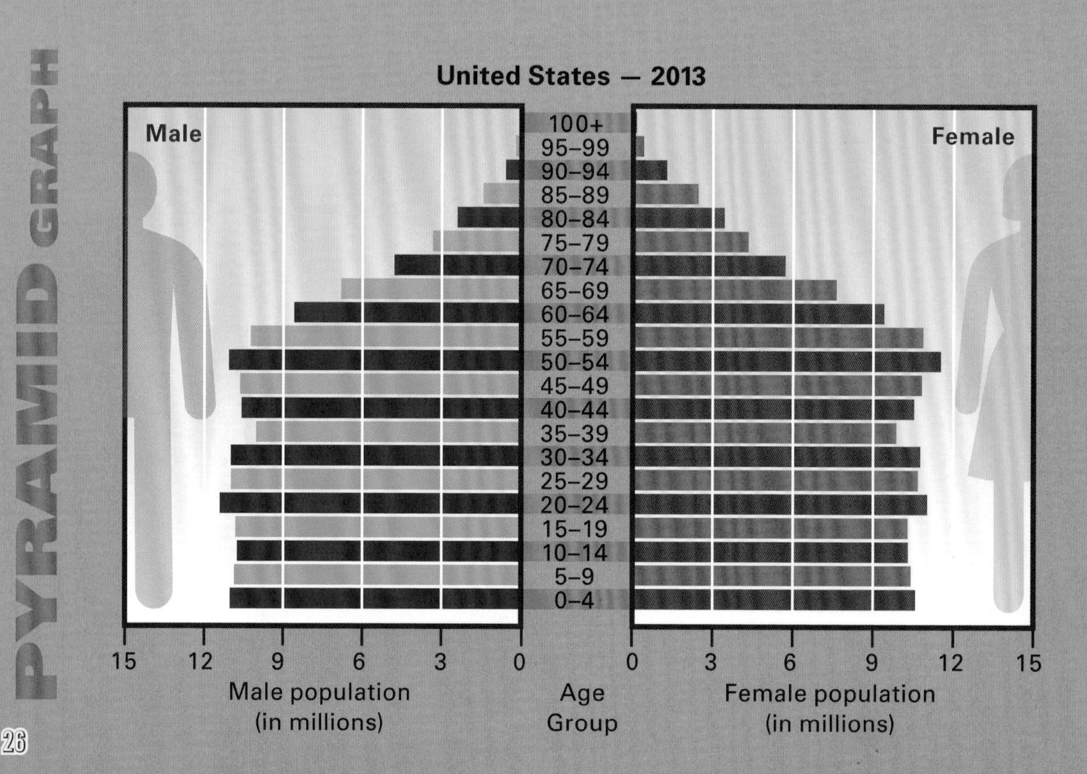

PYRAMID GRAPH

Aging America

With advances in medicine and public health, Americans are living longer than ever. By 2050, one out of five will likely be 65 years or older.

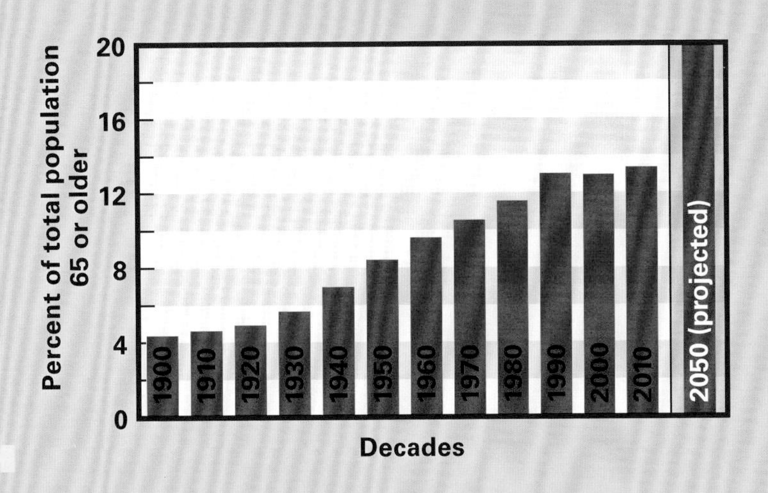

BAR GRAPH

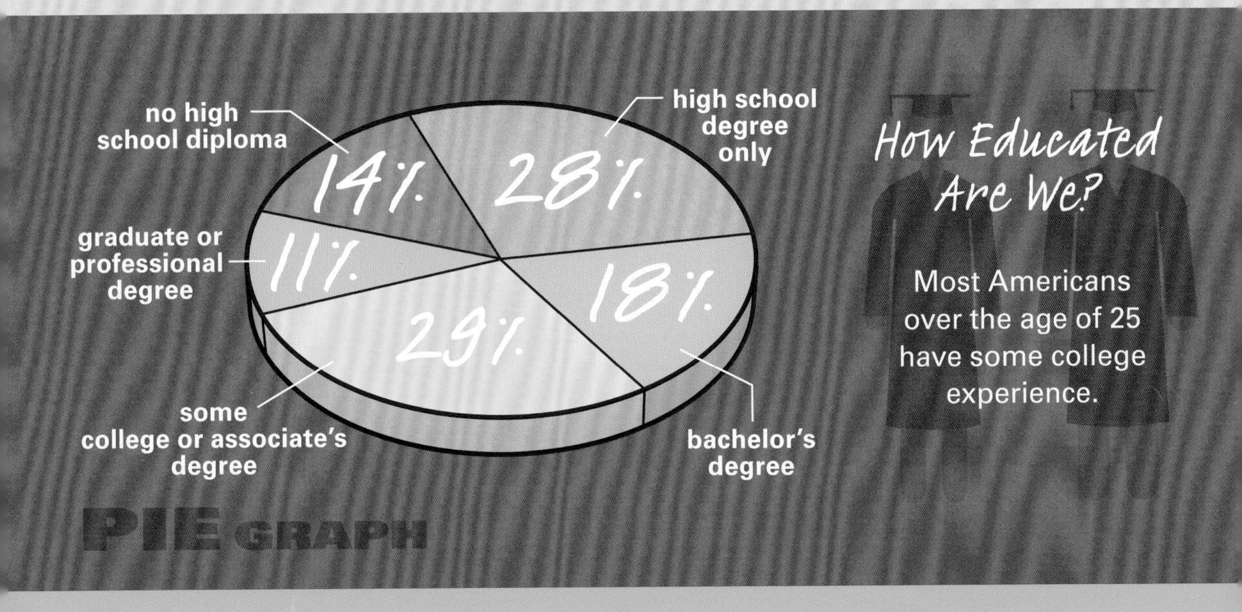

More Degrees for All Races

The percentage of kids who quit school is steadily going down. High school dropout rates have decreased for all races in the past few decades.

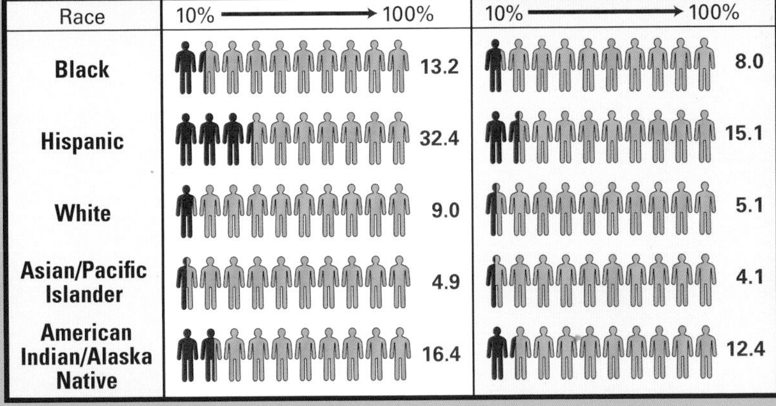

PICTURE GRAPH

ONE DAY IN AMERICA

As the clock ticks around twice each day, check out what goes on in 50 busy states.

TOTAL TAKEOFF

About 2 million people travel on 30,000 flights.

GREEN GONE

US cities lose 11,000 trees to development, disease, natural disasters, and more.

WAY TO GO!

Carpoolers save 223,000 gallons (882,000 liters) of gas in getting around.

SUNNY-SIDE WOW!

Hens on US farms lay about 216 million eggs.

ROCK GAWKERS

About 14,000 people visit the Grand Canyon.

11 10 9 8 7

QUICK ★ FACTS

WAAAAAH!

About 11,000 babies are born.

CRACK AND RUMBLE

More than 200 thunderstorms occur.

PACK IT UP

Moves 'R' Us

About 101,000 people move.

★ QUICK FACTS ★ QUICK FACTS ★

12 1 2 3 4 5 6

WATER WASTERS

Each family uses more than 300 gallons (1,136 liters) of water.

DRIVE TIME

Each adult spends an average of 87 minutes behind the wheel.

tick tick tick tick tick

120 90 30 60

WATER PLEASE!

About 137,000 tons (124,000 metric tons) of salt is mined.

RIP

About 7,000 people die.

Glossary

BARGE: a wide, flat-bottomed boat. Barges are often used for shipping cargo along rivers.

BARRIER ISLAND: a long, thin island that runs in the same direction as a coastline. Barrier islands protect coastlines from storms while hosting unique communities of plants and animals.

CLIMATE CHANGE: changes in Earth's climate patterns caused by changes in average global temperatures. Climate change's effects in the United States include increased drought, downpours, and hurricanes.

DROUGHT: a long period when rainfall is low for a particular area. Drought is one effect of climate change in the United States.

ECOSYSTEM: a community of living things, including their physical surroundings. Plants and animals in an ecosystem depend on one another to survive.

ELEVATION: how high an area of land is compared to sea level. Mount McKinley, Alaska, has the highest elevation in the United States.

ENDANGERED: at risk of dying out. An endangered species has a dangerously low number of members left on the planet.

FOSSIL FUEL: oil, coal, or natural gas. Fossil fuels give off greenhouse gases when they are burned.

GREENHOUSE GAS: one of the gases created by human activity that contributes to the overall warming of the planet. Carbon dioxide is the most common greenhouse gas.

IMMIGRANT: a person who has moved from one country to live in another

IMPORT: to bring in from a foreign country. The United States imports about one-fifth of the fuel it uses.

PLAIN: a large, flat area with few trees. The Great Plains stretch north and south across the central United States.

PLATEAU: a large, raised area that is somewhat flat, like a table

POVERTY: being very poor, according to government standards

SPECIES: a kind of living thing. Members of a species can mate and create offspring.

SUBWAY: an underground train system used for public transportation. New York City has the largest subway system in the world.

TECTONIC PLATE: one of the massive slabs of rock that fit together to form Earth's crust. Moving tectonic plates cause earthquakes.

Further Information

Benoit, Peter. *Climate Change.* New York: Scholastic, 2011.
This book offers solid info on climate change from several angles, including what's being done to fight it.

Discover America
http://www.discoveramerica.com
Not only will this site help you plan your next road trip, but it also lets you read blogs by real travelers about America's best vacation spots.

50States.com
http://www.50states.com
This site can't be beat for basic state facts and trivia.

Higgins, Nadia. *US Culture through Infographics.* Minneapolis: Lerner Publications, 2015.
Explore American people, foods, beliefs, sports, arts, and more in this infographic-packed book.

National Geographic—United States Atlas
http://www.nationalgeographic.com/kids-usa-atlas
Make your own maps, play games, and get state-by-state info at this fun site.

National Park Service
http://www.nps.gov/index.htm
Webcams show real-time views of the Rocky Mountains and other US wonders. This site also has some of the best photos out there.

US Census Bureau—Statistics in Schools
http://www.census.gov/schools/census_for_teens
Did you know 5.7 million US children live with at least one grandparent? Find out more fun population facts at this data site for kids.

US Energy Information Administration—Energy Kids
http://www.eia.gov/kids
More than 50 million homes have three or more TVs. Learn more fun data about our nation's energy habits at this government site for kids.

The Weather Channel—Interactive Weather Map
http://www.weather.com/outlook/weather-news/news/articles/weather-maps_2012-01-13
Click on maps to see just about every kind of weather around the United States.

Expand learning beyond the printed book. Download free, complementary educational resources for this book from our website, www.lerneresource.com.

PHOTO ACKNOWLEDGMENTS
The images in this book are used with the permission of: © Lindsay Douglas /Dreamstime.com, p. 16 (top); Grand Canyon NPS, p. 16 (middle left); NPS Photo/Daniel A. Leifheit, p. 16 (bottom left); NPS Photo/Neal Herbert, p. 16 (bottom right); © iStockphoto.com/Wirepec, p. 17 (top left); © iStockphoto .com/CaptainIFR, p. 17 (top right); Cape Hatteras National Seashore/NPS Photo, p. 17 (middle right); © iStockphoto.com/benkrut, p. 17 (bottom left); © Off Axis Production/Shutterstock.com, p. 17 (bottom right).